YOUR KNOWLEDGE HAS VALUE

AF131208

- We will publish your bachelor's and master's thesis, essays and papers

- Your own eBook and book - sold worldwide in all relevant shops

- Earn money with each sale

Upload your text at www.GRIN.com and publish for free

Bibliographic information published by the German National Library:

The German National Library lists this publication in the National Bibliography; detailed bibliographic data are available on the Internet at http://dnb.dnb.de .

Imprint:

Copyright © 2015 GRIN Verlag, Open Publishing GmbH
Print and binding: Books on Demand GmbH, Norderstedt Germany
ISBN: 9783668463349

This book at GRIN:

http://www.grin.com/en/e-book/367783/the-development-of-women-s-roles-in-germany-since-world-war-ii

Antonia Fischer

The Development of Women's Roles in Germany Since World War II

GRIN Publishing

GRIN - Your knowledge has value

Since its foundation in 1998, GRIN has specialized in publishing academic texts by students, college teachers and other academics as e-book and printed book. The website www.grin.com is an ideal platform for presenting term papers, final papers, scientific essays, dissertations and specialist books.

Visit us on the internet:

http://www.grin.com/

http://www.facebook.com/grincom

http://www.twitter.com/grin_com

Antonia Fischer, 9EM

Development of Women's Roles in Germany beginning from the Post-War Years

Hermann-von-Helmholtz-Gymnasium Europaschule

Facharbeit in Englisch

3. März 2015

Contents

Introduction

"My former husband said: "The man is the protector and the woman is the (maid) servant." " – Mrs X (Due to data privacy I will not release any information on the female interview participant)

It may seem hard to believe, but not too long ago this quote was the reality of most women in Germany. It was self-evident that the woman was inferior to the man. She took care of the household and the children while the man went to work. This is the role women had to play.

Role is a word all too familiar to us. In the dictionary it says: "a part that someone or something has in a particular activity or situation"[1]. One can play the main character in a movie, TV series or a play. One can also play a certain role in everyday life e.g. at home, work and in society in general. The latter is the topic I want to address. In this Facharbeit I want to find out whether the roles of women have or have not changed over time.

It is clear, that women have received more rights in the past. Especially in Germany compared to other countries, since they got to vote already in 1919 as to where in Switzerland they were allowed to vote only in 1971[2]. But what was the woman's role according to society 50 years ago? Nowadays it is completely normal for women to have jobs that are usually viewed as jobs "only for men". But what was it like then?

In the first part of the Facharbeit I want to go into the role of women since the 1950s (the post-war period). This includes the roles of women in the Federal Republic of Germany (FRG) and in the German Democratic Republic (GDR). Subsequently are the current roles of women in Germany described.

In the second part, as my own share of the Facharbeit, I interviewed three females from three different generations. The women were born in the 1930s, in the 1960s and the girl in 1999/2000. All of the questions were asked regarding the time the women were 15 years of age, so the interests would be similar to the girl from my generation. This way it was easier to compare the changes in the roles of women/girls in Germany.

In the end of my Facharbeit I will draw up a summary and therewith conclude and evaluate the role changes.

---

[1] http://www.merriam-webster.com/dictionary/role (accessed on February 10 2015)
[2] Blättel, I. (1989): 70 Jahre Frauenwahlrecht in Deutschland, pp 7-11, in: Informationen für die Frau 1989, Folge 1.

Methodology

Problem Statement

Nowadays, one assumes that gender equity is more or less achieved in Germany. Nevertheless, women and men have different positions in society for example have different roles, identities, and behaviours. These positions have changed over time due to economic, political and socio-cultural development. Changes in gender relationships have taken place in various sectors of society, e.g. in family, neighbourhoods and associations, school and education, at work and in business, but also in more public spheres such as in politics and media.

While the change is assumed to having brought more gender equity, it is questionable, if all sectors of society have had similar achievements. The Facharbeit will answer the question whether roles and identities of women have changed in order to have more gender equity.

Objectives

The aims of the Facharbeit are

- To find out if and how roles and status of women have changed over the course of 60 years.
- To find out in which sectors of society potential changes are most pronounced
- To find out which factors influenced theses changes that might have occurred

In order to reach this aim, several research questions have been formulated that are answered in this Facharbeit:

- How women perceive their role and identity in society now and in the past? Are there changes, and if yes, where and how?
- Which factors do influence the change?
- Which roles and identities haven't changed so much?

Hypotheses

Two main working hypotheses are to be investigated, which are

1. *Women nowadays can work where they want. They are not restricted by cultures and regulations.*
2. *If there has been a change in roles of women in the household, there is also more equality in the household related to care taking activities, even men take over tasks in the household.*

Data Collection

Data collection was done in two ways. First, literature on the history of women's roles and women's movements since the 1950s in Germany was studied. Second, three interviews were conducted with women of three different generations. Each interview lasted approximately one hour. Two interviews were done in German and one in English. The interview guideline is attached in the annex.

Main Part

Role of Women since 1950

At the end of the Second World War the situation of women in Germany was very tough. Not only men but also women feared the retaliation as men as well as women had been politically active during Nazi time and were involved in leading positions. Women, for example, sometimes worked as wardens in concentration camps, even though they were involved to a lesser extent in the Nazi regime than men[3]. Many men were still abroad in war captivity, so the women were on their own. It was their role to clean up and start a new life in the totally destroyed Germany. There was an overflow of 7 million women compared to men [4]. A well-known symbol for the hard life of women in the Post-War period was the Trümmerfrau, which can be translated as "woman who cleared debris after World War II"[5].

The notion of the three K's, which was formed in the Nazi period, was continued after the Second World War. The three K's meaning Kinder (children), Küche (kitchen), Kirche (church) stood for the woman's sole purpose in life[6].

Figure 1 : Trümmerfrauen in East Berlin (Women working in the rubble)

Source: http://www.spiegel.de/fotostrecke/photo-gallery-women-in-the-rubble-fotostrecke-56829-11.html (accessed 9 February 2015)

---

[3] Nave-Herz, Rosemarie (1993): Die Geschichte der Frauenbewegung in Deutschland, Hrsg.: Niedersächsische Landeszentrale für Politische Bildung Hannover, Bonn.
[4] ibid
[5] PONS: http://de.pons.com/übersetzung/deutsch-englisch/Trümmerfrau (accessed 9 February 2015)
[6] Bridenthal, Renate (1973): Beyond Kinder, Küche, Kirche: Weimar Women at Work. Central European History, 6, pp 148-166.

Federal Republic of Germany (FRG) until 1989

After the Second World War, the 3K's model was still dominant in the West German society. In 1949, during the constitution process of the FRG a female parliamentarian fought for the article 3: "Men and women are equal/have equal rights"[7]. The basic idea for an equal society was set, but there was very little evidence, that this ideal view of a society was actually pursued. Real life situation was different, as the marriage and family law was very conservative and was oriented toward the rights of the husband. Married women'were only allowed to work if their husband allowed it. The women's salary was always lower than the men's even if they had the same jobs. Only in 1977 a law passed that allowed both partners, husband and wife, to be active in the labour market and at the same time had to show mutual interest for the duties in the family and the household[8]. As a matter of fact, this didn't turn out to be very successful as there were not enough child caring facilities, and if women actually worked they did this mostly part-time which would allow them to look after the household and the children in the afternoon.

The women's movement in West Germany began "from below", that means it was initiated by the women themselves, because political decision makers did not strongly support the idea of women's emancipation. Women in West Germany since the 1970s fought for equal rights, e.g. equal rights in family, right to abortion, right to divorce[9].

German Democratic Republic (GDR) until 1989

The emancipation of women was one key element of the Socialist Unity Party of Germany (German acronym: SED). The main principle of the GDR was that women could also be freed when women were integrated into the production and work environment[10]. The policy on women's issues was implemented in three phases. The first phase (1946-1965) focused on integrating women in the work life. In 1950 a law was passed to allow women to get maternity leave, access to child care facilities and promotion of working life of women. Also the decision-making power was transferred to both, husband and wife, and not, as it was in the past, the head of the household (the man) made the decisions in the family. The second phase concentrated on advanced training and qualification of women (1963-1972)[11]. Even though women were working, there was still not equity in payment. The image of the East German workingwoman was that of a self-confident, well-educated and successful career

---

[7] Frauenbewegung - der Kampf für Gleichberechtigung: https://www.planet-wissen.de/alltag_gesundheit/frauen/frauenbewegung/index.jsp (accessed 12 February 2015)
[8] Notz, Gisela (2012): Die Geschichte der Frauenbewegungen in Ost- und Westdeutschland, Zeitschrift für Sozialistische Politik und Wissenschaft, http://www.spw.de/data/spw_188_notz.pdf (accessed 12 February 2015).
[9] Lewis, Jone Johnson (1995): Germany - Status of Women, http://womenshistory.about.com/library/ency/blwh_germany_women.htm (accessed on 14 February 2015)
[10] Bütow, Birgit, Heidi Stecker (Hrsg.) (1994): EigenArtige Ostfrauen, Frauenemazipation in der DDR und den neuen Bundesländern, Institut Frau und Gesellschaft, Reihe Theorie und Praxis der Frauenforschung, Band 22, Kleine Verlag, Bielefeld.
[11] Ibid, p.23

woman. Still, women were requested to behave like the good girls they were brought up to be. The third phase (1971-1989) focused on achieving a work-life balance. Many social advantages were given to women to release them from the long working hours and the workload for household duties. A law was passed that women had the right to take a day off every month to do the housekeeping. Later this law was extended to single fathers.[12]

Women in the GDR received numerous chances to develop a different role compared to the former traditional housewife. This was a huge change for this time. Even though the laws to protect women's rights were passed quite early, old values, attitudes and behaviours toward women continued to exist for a longer time.

Present (1989-today)

When Germany was unified in 1989 it did not just merge two halves of a country back together, but also two very different societies. The former FRG and GDR were unlike one another concerning the roles that women played at home and at work. In the GDR more than 90% of women between 15 and 60 were employed, while in FRG this rate was only 60%[13].

During the reunification process old East Germany was forced to adapt to the West German norms and cultures. Even though all societal sectors of East Germany were rearranged, women were affected the most. Many women lost their job, and even more were turned into part-time workers. Many companies were closed and therefore also their day-care facilities[14]. The gender imbalance in this restructuring process is illustrated by the following: By 1995 only 23% of working men had lost their employment, the figure among working women was much higher at 36%[15].

25 years later, the female employment situation in both parts of Germany is similar, though a little bit more employment of women in the East. In 2012, 58% of women had a permanent job in the East, whereas in the West it was 51%.[16]

Gender Development Index

The equality between genders can be seen in numbers with the help of the Gender Development Index, which is based n the Human Development Index (HDI), an index

---

[12] Sachse, C. (2002): Der Hausarbeitstag Gerechtigkeit und Gleichberechtigung in Ost und West 1939-1994. Wallstein Verlag, Göttingen.
[13] FES (2001): Keine Wende am Arbeitsmarkt in Ostdeutschland : eine Zwischenbilanz im Jahre 1996 (Reihe "Wirtschaftspolitische Diskurse" ; 89), Klaus Funken 1996; elektronische Version: FES (Friedrich-Ebert-Stiftung) Library. http://library.fes.de/fulltext/fo-wirtschaft/00323toc.htm (accessed on 12 February 2015)
[14] Lewis, Jone Johnson (1995): Germany - Status of Women, http://womenshistory.about.com/library/ency/blwh_germany_women.htm (accessed on 14 February 2015)
[15] Bonin, H. and Euwal, R. (2002): Participation Behavior of East German Women after German Unification, p.3, http://www.diw.de/documents/dokumentenarchiv/17/39214/bonin_euwals.pdf (accessed on 14 February 2015)
[16] DPA/The Local (14.1.2015): More women work in east than west: Study, http://www.thelocal.de/20150114/female-work-force-stronger-in-east-than-west-study-gdr-ddr (accessed on 14 February 2015)

that is generated every year to compare the human livelihood situation worldwide[17]. The HDI measures three spheres of development, which are

1. a long and healthy life, measured as life expectancy at birth
2. a good knowledge base, measured as adult literacy rate and gross enrolment ratio
3. access to resources to meet a decent standard of living measured as gross domestic product (GDP) per capita

The Gender Development Index disaggregates these main indicators by gender to highlight gender disparities at national level. In the latest report of 2014, 187 countries were included. Germany is ranked 6 after other high-income countries Norway (1), Australia, Switzerland, Netherlands, and the United States (5). Only Norway and the United States are also ranked high in the GDI, while Germany has high disparities between male and female regarding education and income. Therefore it has been ranked only 61 in 2014 (while it has been ranked 20 in previous years). Countries with a relatively high GDI are the Scandinavian, some Latin American and Eastern European countries.

Table 1: Global Gender Gap 2013: List of 14 countries with highest rank

Country	Overall		Economic Participation and Opportunity		Educational Attainment		Health and Survival		Political Empowerment	
	Rank	Score	Rank	Score	Rank	Score	Rank	Score	Rank	Score
Iceland	1	0.8731	22	0.7684	1	1.0000	97	0.9696	1	0.7544
Finland	2	0.8421	19	0.7727	1	1.0000	1	0.9796	2	0.6162
Norway	3	0.8417	1	0.8357	1	1.0000	93	0.9697	3	0.5616
Sweden	4	0.8129	14	0.7829	38	0.9977	69	0.9735	4	0.4976
Philippines	5	0.7832	16	0.7773	1	1.0000	1	0.9796	10	0.3760
Ireland	6	0.7823	29	0.7450	34	0.9988	65	0.9737	6	0.4115
New Zealand	7	0.7799	15	0.7797	1	1.0000	93	0.9697	12	0.3703
Denmark	8	0.7779	25	0.7639	1	1.0000	64	0.9739	11	0.3738
Switzerland	9	0.7736	23	0.7681	66	0.9919	72	0.9733	16	0.3610
Nicaragua	10	0.7715	91	0.6218	28	0.9996	55	0.9758	5	0.4889
Belgium	11	0.7684	34	0.7367	67	0.9918	47	0.9787	14	0.3664
Latvia	12	0.7610	17	0.7767	1	1.0000	1	0.9796	26	0.2875
Netherlands	13	0.7608	26	0.7592	44	0.9954	93	0.9697	22	0.3191
Germany	14	0.7583	46	0.7120	86	0.9818	49	0.9780	15	0.3611

Source: World Economic Forum 2013

The World Economic Forum has initiated another gender index in 2006, the so-called Global Gender Gap Index (see Table 1), to track progress and developments in

---

[17] UNDP (2014): Human Development Report 2014: Sustaining Human Progress: reducing Vulnerabilities and Building Resilience, http://hdr.undp.org/en/rethinking-work-for-human-development (accessed on 9 February 2015)

gender disparities among nations[18]. It is based on four pillars: Economic Participation and Opportunity, Educational Attainment, Health and Survival and Political Empowerment. Table 1 shows Germany with its rank 14 out of 136 countries. Political empowerment, which is measured as ratio of females with seats in parliament over male value, the ratio of females at ministerial level over male value, and the years of female head of states over male value is ranked with 15 at higher level. Sweden in comparison is on rank 4 in the political empowerment subcategory. It shows very high gender balance in the parliament, in which almost 45% of the members are female[19].

Cases of three generations: roles, identity and behaviour of women
In this part of the Facharbeit follow the results of the conducted interviews of three women from three different generations.

Adolescence and young adulthood (15 years) between 1950 and 1975
Mrs X is 78 years old. When she was 15 her younger brother was 13 years old. Her mother took care of the household, while her father went to work. The kids didn't really help in the household. They mostly did their schoolwork. Mrs X sometimes helped her mother press duvet covers. Her brother didn't help in the household, which was typical for boys. The children had very little to say in the household. If they wanted to have some food out of the fridge, they had to ask for permission first.

At the age of 15, Mrs X went to an all girls' school. During breaks she talked to her girlfriends about actors they liked.

Her first boyfriend was the son of the neighbours, whom she often went biking with. Even though their parents knew each other, her parents didn't really approve of their relationship. They thought she should wait to have a boyfriend until she was planning on getting married. Having a relationship with a boy at such a young age was very unusual at that point in time.

Mrs X had one female and one male role model. The female role model was Audrey Hepburn, whom she dressed like, because she admired her. She stood for beauty, youthfulness and independence. In "Roman Holiday" she broke out of a castle and did things that were impossible for a princess to do. This is what Mrs X very much identified herself with. The male role model or male celebrity she liked was Clark Gable from "Gone with the Wind". He stood for masculine strength. He would catch you when you fell, he would protect you, he would lead you, he would always be there, and would help you with decisions. Mrs X was looking for a man, who offered protection and stability, which was very typical for her generation. The woman was

---

[18] World Economic Forum (2013): The Global Gender Gap Index 2013.
http://www3.weforum.org/docs/WEF_GenderGap_Report_2013.pdf (accessed on 27 February 2015)
[19] ibid, p. 21.

perceived to be the weaker one in the relationship, which her parents exemplified to her.

Mrs X never imagined anything other than starting a family and being a housewife in her future. Her father already had plans about what kind of job he wanted her to do. When she left school at the age of 16, he signed her up to pursue an apprenticeship in an insurance company without having asked her beforehand. She didn't want to act on the suggestion from her father and talked to her boyfriend. He proposed her to go to a school of interpreting in Munich. She then told her parents where she wanted to go instead of the insurance company. They said: "But we already saved your dowry. We cannot pay your school fee." They had a hope chest where they had collected bed linen, tablecloths, her silver cutlery et cetera for her. They always thought she was going to marry someday and therefore she needed what was called "dowry". It was a supply of things that one needs at the beginning of a marriage. Mrs X was speechless when she heard her parents had made such a decision without her knowing. According to Mrs X the future of most young women was determined by the parent's decisions and actions. But then her parents reluctantly allowed her to go to this school of interpreting.

She believes nowadays girls in Germany can be more independent and have more decision making power. They also have more responsibilities. Then, women depended on their husbands. In society, women only had a value if they had a man at their side. The time where Mrs X was raised was a really restrictive time for girls. They were forced to grow into a certain direction, as a housewife and servant for their husbands.

Adolescence and young adulthood (15 years) between 1975 and 2000
Mrs Y is 47 years old. When she was 15 her younger brother was 13 years old. During the day her father went to work, while her mother stayed at home and took care of the household. The kids had to help around the house. Both of them had to dust the house and help weed the garden. They helped with what they could do well. Her brother repaired things, but was also good at ironing, which is why he had to do that as well. Mrs Y was good at baking, so she had to bake cakes and other meals. Her tasks were typical for a girl, because girls worked a lot at home. It was less typical for that time that her brother had to help in the house.

After school, Mrs Y did Jazz dancing, which was only for girls. She played volleyball, where both girls and boys participated. She also was a scout, where she was mostly among boys since it was untypical for a girl to participate.

She didn't have specific role models, but she liked girls who stood for independence e.g. Alex Owens from "Flashdance". Mrs Y was an untypical girl since she was not so much into clothing and hair.

She always wanted to have children, but also always wanted to travel abroad. She didn't want to become a housewife. A lot of girls she knew wanted to see the world and go away from home. Lots of her girlfriends became stewardesses. Combining both was not an easy task, as her husband and other friends were convinced that childcare is mainly up to the woman.

She believes teenagers from her generation were much more free compared to teens nowadays. Parents were not so scared about their youngsters. Also there were many different youth cultures and groups then, e.g. punks, hippies, bikers. Nowadays all teenage girls dress and look the same. In the 80's, girls were not obsessed with being thin. They had more free time and space to develop. Teenage girls nowadays have a pretty stressful life. Due to social media usage, teenage girls feel like they have to look like celebrities.

On the positive side, she mentions, that the adolescents in 2015 appreciate the value of family. When she was young, a lot of girls didn't want to have a family, because they wanted to explore the world. Nowadays it is easier for women to have children and pursue a career at the same time. The society is much more family-friendly, as it offers childcare facilities. Then, the mothers didn't work and instead took care of the kids. The fact that her mother didn't work pushed her to pursue a career and have kids. She didn't want to wait until she found a husband that cared for her.

Her mathematics teacher once said: "Of course you don't understand mathematics. You are a girl. It's self-evident that you don't understand it". These sorts of statements were typical for teachers. Especially science and mathematics teachers believed natural sciences were nothing girls should concern themselves with.

Adolescence (14 years) between 2000 and 2015
Ms Z is 14 years old and lives in a family with her parents and her younger brother (12). She doesn't have many tasks around the house, she believes. Ms Z only has to do the tasks that are normal for a girl her age. She does most of these chores together with her brother, whom she loves very much. These duties include putting the dishes into the dishwasher, vacuuming the house, cooking as a family and setting the table. If her parents have a lot to do the children sometimes have to do more, like preparing the meals or going grocery shopping. Given the fact she lives in the house with her parents, the least she could do is give them a hand when they need it. She said, one girl once told her that she had to watch her younger sister and got money for it from her parents. That is superfluous and should not be expected of parents.

Girls and boys, Ms Z believes, have a friendly and companionable relation. They talk and sometimes tease each other, but there is no feeling of inferiority to one of the genders. Also it is normal for a boy and a girl to meet, regardless if out of romantic reasons or not.

After school Ms Z plays the flute, writes, goes swimming and goes horse riding. She believes these activities as well as meeting friends, going shopping, eating with friends, walking the dog, riding the bike, going to the cinema, and sometimes cooking or baking are all activities typical for a girl in 2015.

Ms Z's male role model is a singer from the band Sunrise Avenue "Samu Haber". He stands for good looks and funniness. She admires that he never stopped doing what he likes (singing) and how he worked his way up.

In the future Ms Z wants a nice husband, whom she loves, a little house with a garden, two children, and a job. Most of all, she wants to be happy and stay in contact with her brother and her parents. She wants to go into politics or economics. She wants a fair balance regarding the household. Both her and her partner should have equal jobs concerning taking care of the kids and the household. Also, she wants to be able to go to work, because the worst thing that could happen to her is if she became a housewife. Taking care of the house would be boring for her. She keeps thinking of the future and says if her and her husband ever split, she would end up with nothing, because all she had ever done was taking care of the household. The role of a housewife would make her feel inferior to her husband.

When I asked her how she thinks the roles of women in Germany have changed she answered that 50 years ago women would have become housewives without earning money. Most women would have liked to find a rich husband who would have bought them everything they wanted and with whom they would have had many children. She told the story of how her great aunt, who is now 70 years old, never married which is the reason for people looking at her with estrangement.

In 2015, girls have to be good looking. They have to wear discreet make-up and wear short and tight clothing. "The shorter the better" she says. Girls from the age 10 already do this. For her it is a big challenge, as she is not convinced that good looks and sexy outfits are the most important things in the world.

Conclusion

Women at work

Hypothesis: *Women nowadays can work where they want. They are not restricted by cultures and regulations.*

The findings from the Internet and literal research and the interviews support my working hypothesis. German women have gained a lot of rights during the course of 50 years, from the right to work without their husband's permissions, to the right to abortion. In the 1950s it was normal for the husband to go to work and for the wife to take care of the household, which was confirmed by Mrs X and my research e.g. the three Ks. Also in the 80s the woman still took care of the household. Finally in 2015, a lot of women pursue a career and there are many in higher positions in politics e.g. Germany's first female chancellor Angela Merkel.

Sharing household and care taking chores

Hypothesis: *If there has been a change in roles of women in the household, there is also more equality in the household related to care taking activities. Even men take over tasks in the household.*

My findings support this hypothesis as well. In the 1950s, in the generation of Mrs X, it was unthinkable for a boy or a man to help in the household. This was the job of the woman. In the 1980s, in the family of Mrs Y the little brother helped in the household, but this was still a very unusual case. Nowadays, in 2015, it is completely normal for both genders to help in the household. The family cooks together, sets the table and the parents take turns taking care of the children. In terms of household, I believe equity has been achieved. There are even families where the wife goes to work and the husband stays at home to take care of the children and the household. Nevertheless, housework is not an activity that is looked up to. As seen in the interview of Ms Z, a lot of girls would not want to become a housewife, because not only would they find it boring and feel useless, but also feel a notion of inferiority towards the man.

I believe girls in 2015 want to keep themselves all options open, so they have enough room for development. They want to explore the world and all it has to offer. Deciding to become a housewife could mean missing out on things, if the sole purpose in life would be to find a husband, get married, have children and take care of the household. Because of the history of women's roles as housewives, there is always the risk of falling back into the role of a woman 50 years ago.

Since women give birth to children, there will always be a time in their life when they have to be more at home to take care of the children and are therefore more challenged in the household. In order for them not to be excluded from the labour market, there should be more family-friendly facilities like there were in the GDR, where there were childcare facilities provided by the employer. This would aid the woman during the time of her life where she must dedicate more time to family instead of work. By helping her, she would not be forced to leave the labour market or her job in order to start a family.

Annex

References

Books

1. Blättel, I. (1989): 70 Jahre Frauenwahlrecht in Deutschland, pp 7-11, in: Informationen für die Frau 1989, Folge 1.
2. Bridenthal, Renate (1973): Beyond Kinder, Küche, Kirche: Weimar Women at Work. Central European History, 6, pp 148-166.
3. Bütow, Birgit, Heidi Stecker (Hrsg.) (1994): EigenArtige Ostfrauen, Frauenemanzipation in der DDR und den neuen Bundesländern, Institut Frau und Gesellschaft, Reihe Theorie und Praxis der Frauenforschung, Band 22, Kleine Verlag, Bielefeld.
4. Nave-Herz, Rosemarie (1993): Die Geschichte der Frauenbewegung in Deutschland, Hrsg.: Niedersächsische Landeszentrale für Politische Bildung Hannover, Bonn.
5. Sachse, C. (2002): Der Hausarbeitstag Gerechtigkeit und Gleichberechtigung in Ost und West 1939-1994. Wallstein Verlag, Göttingen.

Images

1. http://www.spiegel.de/fotostrecke/photo-gallery-women-in-the-rubble-fotostrecke-56829-11.html (accessed 9 February 2015)

Internet Sources

1. Bonin, H. and Euwal, R. (2002): Participation Behavior of East German Women after German Unification, p.3, http://www.diw.de/documents/dokumentenarchiv/17/39214/bonin_euwals.pdf (accessed on 14 February 2015)
2. DPA/The Local (14.1.2015): More women work in east than west: Study, http://www.thelocal.de/20150114/female-work-force-stronger-in-east-than-west-study-gdr-ddr (accessed on 14 February 2015)
3. FES (2001): Keine Wende am Arbeitsmarkt in Ostdeutschland : eine Zwischenbilanz im Jahre 1996 (Reihe "Wirtschaftspolitische Diskurse" ; 89), Klaus Funken 1996; elektronische Version: FES (Friedrich-Ebert-Stiftung) Library. http://library.fes.de/fulltext/fo-wirtschaft/00323toc.htm (accessed on 12 February 2015)
4. Frauenbewegung - der Kampf für Gleichberechtigung: https://www.planet-wissen.de/alltag_gesundheit/frauen/frauenbewegung/index.jsp (accessed on 12 February 2015)
5. Lewis, Jone Johnson (1995): Germany - Status of Women, http://womenshistory.about.com/library/ency/blwh_germany_women.htm (accessed on 14 February 2015)
6. Merriam-Webster: http://www.merriam-webster.com/dictionary/role. (accessed on 10 February 2015).

7. Notz, Gisela (2012): Die Geschichte der Frauenbewegungen in Ost- und Westdeutschland, Zeitschrift für Sozialistische Politik und Wissenschaft, http://www.spw.de/data/spw_188_notz.pdf. (accessed on 12 February 2015).
8. PONS: http://de.pons.com/übersetzung/deutsch-englisch/Trümmerfrau. (accessed on 9 February 2015).
9. UNDP (2014): Human Development Report 2014: Sustaining Human Progress: reducing Vulnerabilities and Building Resilience, http://hdr.undp.org/en/rethinking-work-for-human-development (accessed on 9 February 2015)
10. World Economic Forum (2013): The Global Gender Gap Index 2013. http://www3.weforum.org/docs/WEF_GenderGap_Report_2013.pdf (accessed on 27 February 2015)

Alle persönlichen Daten werden vertraulich behandelt und bis auf das Alter und das Geschlecht werden keine Informationen an die Öffentlichkeit preisgegeben. Vielen Dank für die Teilnahme an diesem Interview!

The main aim of the interview is to find out how the roles of women in German society have changed over time. This analysis is done according to three different sectors in society: family, education and community.

The whole interview questions are asked concerning your life as a young girl at the age of 15.

1. How was your family constellation set up? Did you have siblings? If yes how many?
2. What was your role in the house (compared to your siblings)? What were your major responsibilities around the house? How did you feel about that? Was this a typical job for you?
3. What was typical for boys/girls during school breaks? Games, girl/boy things etc.
4. What relation did you/girls in general have to guys?
5. What sort of (after school) activities did you participate in? Were these activities typical for a girl at that time?
6. When you were young who were your female/male role models? (Books, movies, teachers) What did she/he stand for?
7. What did you want to be/have when you grew up regarding family situation and work? What dreams did you have?
8. If you were a teenage girl nowadays, what do you think would be different to your former life considering role models, job wishes, family and community (e.g. activities)?
9. In which field of life (family, education, community) did you experience discrimination against girls or guys?